Original title:
Jewels and Journeys

Copyright © 2025 Creative Arts Management OÜ
All rights reserved.

Author: Maxwell Donovan
ISBN HARDBACK: 978-1-80586-114-0
ISBN PAPERBACK: 978-1-80586-586-5

Echoes of Discovery

In a land where shiny rocks do gleam,
We set off to chase a silly dream.
With pickaxes made from kitchen spoons,
Finding treasures beneath the monsoon.

A crab danced by, with a shiny shell,
Was it a prize? We couldn't quite tell.
'Is that a diamond?' one friend did shout,
Nope, just a gum wrapper, time to head out!

The ground shook! Was it gold?
But nope, a potato, grand and old.
We laughed and played, just like kids,
Turns out, it's the journey that truly bids.

A Quest for Brilliance

Off we marched with silly hats,
Searching for glittering, shiny spats.
But all we found were socks and shoes,
Boring rocks? Nah, these are clues!

The old man claimed he had the might,
To lift a stone that glowed so bright.
We waited and waited, what would he find?
Just a pizza box, oh how unkind!

A raccoon dug in, wearing a crown,
With pizza slices he offered us down.
'Is the treasure of wisdom really this?'
We learned to laugh, and that's pure bliss!

Celestial Stones

Stars shined bright, but we looked below,
For twinkling things only we'd know.
But off we tripped in the grass so tall,
Found shiny buttons! I'd call that a haul!

We met a cat with a sparkly collar,
She sneezed at our stash and called us a scholar.
'You think these baubles are worth a dime?'
But her purr was treasure, oh so sublime!

A frog joined in, gave us his advice,
'Quit chasing shiny! Just take some rice!'
With laughter we feasted, our spirits soared,
Turns out, real wealth's just never bored!

The Quartz Chronicles

Once upon a time in a dusty land,
We sought out glitters, our hearts were grand.
Slipping on sandals, we began to roam,
Scraping our knees, still far from home.

We found a rock shaped like a shoe,
And named it Fred, our lucky view.
'Let's take it back, it's quite bizarre!'
But on the way, we lost our car!

We hiked for hours, through mud and muck,
'Today's just a blast!' said my friend with luck.
In the end, found treasures of laughter and grace,
Who needs the shiny, in this wild, crazy space!

Captured Light in Every Step

In a backpack full of trinkets,
I tripped over my own two feet,
Each glimmer brought a chuckle,
As I scrambled for a seat.

My map was upside down,
A compass spinning wild,
Yet every path I ventured,
Left me somehow beguiled.

The sun peeked through the trees,
Winking as I lost my way,
With each shimmering misstep,
I danced a bright ballet.

I found a coin from ages past,
And thought it must be fate,
Turns out it was just a button,
From my pants—now that's first-rate!

The Quest for Dazzling Dreams

Setting off with a grill and gear,
My dreams were bold and bright,
But as I packed my sandwiches,
I forgot the drink—oh fright!

Chasing sparkles in the distance,
I thought I'd find a throne,
Instead I met a squirrel,
Who claimed it as his own.

With each step in this adventure,
I stumbled on a shoe,
It looked like someone's treasure,
But smelled like morning dew.

The glitter followed like a shadow,
As I laughed across the land,
Who knew a quest for brilliance,
Could leave me quite so tanned!

Sparkling Reflections of the Past

I found a mirror by the lake,
Thinking it would show my grace,
It cracked up at my breakfast,
And splashed me in the face!

An old trunk full of memories,
With dust and bits of lace,
Glimmering with laughter shared,
In every goofy space.

A photo of me, all dressed up,
In socks that didn't match,
The sparkle of my childhood,
Now a shiny game of catch.

With each twinkle of the sunset,
I hugged my past so tight,
In the reflection of the water,
My goofy grin took flight!

Navigating Through Prismatic Winds

The breeze blew colors left and right,
I squinted at the sky,
Mixing rainbows into bubbles,
As I tried not to fly.

A map made of rainbow stickers,
Only led me in a spin,
Each step inside this windy maze,
Had me grinning with chagrin.

I shouted at the swirling hues,
"Just show me where to go!"
But as the wind-tossed me about,
I learned to take it slow.

At last, I found a treasure chest,
Full of laughter—what a find!
With every swirl of colored gusts,
I twirled with peace of mind!

An Expedition of Elegance

In a quest for shiny things, they roam,
With hats too big, off they go from home.
Finding bling on every street,
But trip over shoes, oh what a feat!

The map is upside down and a mess,
They laugh so hard, who needs success?
Sparkly customs at every turn,
But they forget what they came to learn!

The Dazzling Journey

With sparkle toothpaste and bright, gold spray,
They set off at dawn, oh what a day!
Chasing glimmers, chasing giggles,
On a road of twists, they dance and wiggle.

Each corner turns a story bright,
A lost shoe in a tangle, what a sight!
Laughing till they can't catch their breath,
Ah, such fun—no fear of death!

Spectrums of Adventure

Wearing socks with sandals, quite a bold sight,
They venture through valleys, oh what a flight!
Collecting odd trinkets, a fern or two,
Is that a gem? No, just some goo!

Hiking up hills with a glittery hat,
They stumble on rocks, now, how 'bout that?
Pockets full of nonsense, what a haul,
Radiant laughter is the best of all!

Luminous Liaisons

The friends met for brunch, with plates all a-mess,
Why wear pearls when you can wear dress?
With laughter exploding over toast so grand,
A sprinkle of chaos, as they all planned.

They set out for fun, a parade of delight,
Each step filled with giggles, oh what a sight!
In a world full of colors, so bold and bright,
Who needs shiny things when you have a bite?

Resplendent Sights at Every Turn

Wandered down the silly street,
With shiny rocks beneath my feet.
A ladybird in diamond shades,
Telling tales of glimmering parades.

I tripped on glitter, oh what a scene,
As rainbows danced, so bright and keen.
My pockets jingle, full of bling,
A playful twist to any fling!

A Voyage of Shining Moments

On a boat made of candy wraps,
I sailed through stormy giggle traps.
The captain, a parrot, dressed so bright,
With golden feathers, a comical sight!

He squawked about treasures hidden well,
While I just chuckled, casting my spell.
The ocean sparkled with silly pride,
As I rode the waves on this wacky ride!

Gemstone Trails

I found a path of sparkling crumbs,
Leading to a place where laughter hums.
A garden gnome with a ruby nose,
Told knock-knock jokes as the wind blows.

Down the trail, I met a fox,
With emerald socks and a pair of crocs.
He danced around in a goofy trance,
In this land of whimsy, we took a chance!

Radiant Paths

A rainbow slide down a sparkling hill,
Where unicorns twirl and space-time still.
Each moment beams, a laughter spree,
With twilight giggles in wild decree.

I met a snail with a diamond shell,
Who boasted tales, oh so swell.
Racing the clouds, we tripped and rolled,
In this radiant quest for fun untold!

Crystals of Experience Underfoot

Stepping on marbles, oh what a sight,
I trip on a pebble, roll left, then right.
Mismatched socks, who knew they could dance?
Life's little tumbles, fate does enhance.

Collecting odd treasures, my pockets overflow,
A button, a feather, and a spare glow.
Each funny mishap, a memory bright,
Like a jester in shoes that are two sizes light.

Whispers of Brilliant Destinations

Maps upside down, I wander with glee,
Following birds who seem lost like me.
A café where coffee tastes just like sand,
Oh, the adventures that fate has planned!

Crossing a bridge made of bubbles and dreams,
I slip on a banana, or so it seems.
With laughter erupting from every slip,
My journey's a comedy, a wild road trip.

Glistening Turns in the Odyssey

Around every corner, a new twist awaits,
My GPS speaks in riddles and fates.
Found a hedgehog stuck in a pie,
He offered me wisdom, or was that just rye?

With shoelaces tangled, I make my way,
Grinning at mischief that colors my day.
Wobbling onward, I trip and I swerve,
In this circus of life, it's giggles I serve.

Adorned by the Stars Above

Stargazing is tricky when clouds play a game,
A comet's a fish hook, fun how they came.
I wear my dreams like a crown on my head,
Each sparkle a giggle, each twinkle a thread.

Chasing my hat through a whirlwind of fun,
It flutters and dances like it's on the run.
Under the moonlight, all mischief is fair,
Every glimmering laugh, a potion to share.

Crystalline Quest

In a cave deep and dark, I found a surprise,
A shiny rock that sparkled and lied,
I thought it was gold, but took a closer look,
Turns out it was just my lunchbox inside.

With a map full of scribbles and a compass that spins,
I took an odd turn, right where it begins,
My friends laughed so hard at my wobbly stride,
They said, "Just follow the glitter and shine!"

On a hill made of sand, there's treasure to claim,
A pile of old buttons, we'll start a new game,
We'll dress like pirates and sail through the air,
And sing shanties of nonsense, without a care.

So here's to the fun of missteps we make,
Collecting the nonsense, for laughter's sake,
In a whimsical chase for things that we find,
Life's quirks are the treasures that tickle the mind.

The Emerald Expedition

Off on a trip with my floppy old hat,
I searched for a treasure—imagine that!
But found only socks, most mismatched and torn,
My expedition felt less shiny, more worn.

In a forest of giggles, a bubblegum tree,
Grew candy-coated dreams, just waiting for me,
I bounced on my toes, with a snicker and cheer,
Who knew that sweet bounty would soon disappear?

My GPS blinked like a disco at night,
It led me in circles, oh what a sight,
I tripped on a twig and fell in a stream,
My quest for the sparkles had turned to a dream.

Yet through all the mischief, the slips and the slides,
I laughed at the madness, with friends by my sides,
Who needs gems when you've made such a crew?
The richest of riches are the giggles we knew.

Glittering Footprints

With shoes made of glitter, I danced down the lane,
Sprinkling my sparkles like a pop star in rain,
But stumbled on puddles, oh what a splash,
My journey looked like a confetti mad dash.

On the road of bright colors, I found a lost shoe,
It belonged to a cat who claimed it was blue,
We wandered together, causing a scene,
Furry feline fashion in a world so serene.

I met a wild squirrel, who thought he was grand,
He wore tiny sunglasses and called his own band,
We jammed in the meadow, where laughter took flight,
And left shiny footprints that twinkled so bright.

So cheer for the moments of slip and of trip,
With sparkles and giggles, let's embrace every flip,
For in this grand quest, it's the fun that we keep,
As we dance through the chaos, in laughter we leap.

A Tapestry of Light

In a land where the rainbows just tripped on the sun,
I gathered up sparkles, oh what silly fun,
With a brush full of colors, I painted the air,
Every stroke was a giggle, no sorrow to bear.

Chasing the shadows, the curls of the glow,
I tumbled through laughter, a shimmering show,
Bumping into rainbows, they jived in a flare,
A tapestry woven with giggles to share.

I hid in a flower, to play peek-a-boo,
But a butterfly giggled and swatted me too,
As I rolled through the daisies, a dance in full flight,
We twirled like the wind, in our playful delight.

At the end of the day, when the sky turned to night,
I giggled and twinkled, feeling all right,
For the sparkles that matter aren't those made of stone,
But the laughter and joy that we find on our own.

A Mosaic of Glimmers

A trinket fell from a pocket,
It rolled right under a sock,
Found by the cat in a frenzy,
He thought it was his new rock.

A button, a bead, and a thimble,
All stuck in the couch's embrace,
Mom's treasure is now a jungle,
With wild googly eyes on the face.

A lost dime danced in the sun,
Chasing a fly without care,
Suddenly it caught a glimpse,
Of a toddler with sticky hair.

The treasures we find in the mess,
Make ordinary things feel so bright,
Every sparkle is a funny jest,
In our laughter, a colorful light.

Celestial Caravan

An old shoe flew through the air,
It landed with quite a big thud,
The dog thought it was a fair prize,
A treasure hidden in the mud.

A shiny rock caught my brother's eye,
He bargained for it with a smile,
But it turned out to be just plain clay,
That took us hours to compile.

We packed our bags full of odd things,
With hopes of finding great thrills,
But all we discovered was grandma's cheese,
And socks with very strange frills.

Riding high on comedic glows,
Our caravan squeaked like a toy,
Each stop a mishap, joyfully grows,
In laughter, we find our true joy.

The Journey of a Thousand Hues

A rainbow spilled out from my bag,
In colors that sparked silly dreams,
But it turned into puddles of paint,
And my mom yelled, 'Don't ruin the beams!'

I followed a butterfly wearing shades,
It led me to munch on wild cake,
But all I found was a sleepy frog,
As it snorted and awoke with a shake.

With a group of pals, we made our way,
To find a golden treasure chest,
But it was filled with gum and toys,
The fun had truly been the best!

So off we skipped, our hearts aglow,
Each step a giggle, each mile a laugh,
Wrapped in joy, as colors flow,
Creating memories that will outlast.

A Crystal Ballad

In the attic, I found a glass ball,
I thought it would tell me my fate,
But it just sat there, silent and clear,
And invited the dust bunnies to sate.

A mirror, a glint, and a jester's hat,
Sitting upon the same shelf,
Reflected my double chin and jokes,
As I laughed with my tiny self.

The "sorcerer" wore my dad's old socks,
As he waved a wand made of spoons,
He tried to conjure a sparkling snack,
But the fridge just hummed old tunes.

Our ballad of crystals sparkled bright,
As we tripped over laughter and light,
Each charm a giggle, each jest a delight,
We danced 'til the stars bid us goodnight.

Beyond the Diamond Veil

In a land where sparkles dance,
My map's made of shiny pants.
I tripped on a ruby's glow,
And fell into a wig of snow.

A squirrel stole my golden spoon,
Claimed it's his to eat at noon.
I chased him down a zany path,
While laughing in a sparkly laugh.

Underneath a sapphire sky,
I tried to wave a passing guy.
He slipped on a garnet slick,
And shouted, 'Man, this trip's too quick!'

Each rock I found was quite bizarre,
One wobbled like a dancing star.
I packed my bag with all my sights,
Then dropped my snacks—what a fright!

But fortune hides in silly places,
With wobbly gems and silly faces.
So let us roam, from coast to coast,
For laughter is what we love most.

Prism of Wanderlust

Off we go with bags of glitch,
To places where the fools may twitch.
I wore a hat that sparkled bright,
Swore it glowed with sheer delight.

Found a trail of funky shoes,
Each step adorned with funny hues.
I stepped in yellow, tripped in green,
And rolled through bushes all unseen.

A parrot perched upon my head,
Cawed about a cake I dread.
It flung a cupcake, oh what bliss,
And I sang loud—who could resist?

With a wink and a silly dance,
I chased a glimmer, thought I'd prance.
But it led me down to a creek,
Where frogs croaked out their cantankerous peak.

But oh, what gems I found in muck,
A shiny penny, what a luck!
In muddy battles, laughter's born,
As we travel through the thorny corn.

Radiance in Transit

I boarded a train that waved like pie,
With windows that winked and said bye-bye.
My ticket's a cookie, oh what fun,
But crumbs went flying—oh, the run!

A lady with pearls tried to scold,
Said my snacking was far too bold.
But I smiled and offered her a bite,
Now we're both snacks in sheer delight.

Between the sips of fizzy drinks,
We plotted a heist of goofy prinks.
The snack cart had more jewels than gold,
We laughed till our secrets were all told.

So on this journey rich in cheer,
We've made friends, oh dear, oh dear!
Let's toast to each silly adventure,
With sparkling drinks that taste like treasure!

The Garnet Expedition

In harness made of sequined thread,
I led a quest that nearly fled.
With maps of jokes in every fold,
We searched for treasures more than gold.

Our leader claimed to have a plan,
But tripped on his own silly span.
He bounced off rocks in pure delight,
Our laughter echoed through the night.

A cat in shades joined our fun,
Declared that we should run and run.
With tails and sparkles, we took flight,
Through jungles where the trees were bright.

Each stumble left a gem behind,
From gooey globs that were hard to find.
But in pursuit of glimmering fun,
We realized our laughter's never done.

The Celestial Quest

In a land of shiny bling,
A squirrel found a golden ring.
He danced with glee, a silly sight,
Chasing shadows, late at night.

A raccoon joined with flair and zest,
Proposing they both take a quest.
With peanut butter as their prize,
They journeyed under starlit skies.

Through fields of glitter, across the stream,
They saw a disco ball that gleamed.
The moonlight spun a wild dance,
As critters joined in their trance.

They laughed and tripped, all in a whirl,
Under the spell of the glitzy pearl.
For treasure isn't always gold,
Sometimes it's fun and laughter told.

Paths of Radiance

Two hedgehogs in bow ties so bright,
Set out to chase the dawn's first light.
With mismatched socks and shoes askew,
They looked like stars in a circus zoo.

A trail of sparkles, so they thought,
Was leading them to riches they sought.
Yet when they reached the glowing gate,
They found it led to a dancing plate.

Pies flew past in a blueberry storm,
As giggles erupted in silly form.
They rolled and tumbled, grinning wide,
In the land of laughter, they took a ride.

When evening fell, they shared a snack,
Giggling over how to get back.
With stars above as their guiding light,
Their real treasure was the sheer delight.

Glints of an Odyssey

A clumsy goat in a shiny cape,
Set out to build a glorious escape.
But on the way, he slipped and spun,
Landing headfirst in a pie of fun.

His friends, the sheep, they gathered round,
To witness the plop with leaps and bound.
With woolly laughter, they rolled in glee,
For true adventure is silly and free.

An owl perched high, with serious face,
Shouted wisdom from his secret place.
"Don't chase the sparkles, or shiny sights,
Enjoy the laughter, the joyous nights!"

So they pranced and danced, their fears all gone,
With every clatter, the silliness shone.
For amidst the glints and playful schemes,
They found the joy that fuels their dreams.

The Illumined Trail

On a trail lit by winking stars,
A penguin danced with guitars.
He slid on ice with style and grace,
While chasing shadows all over the place.

A snail in shades tried to keep pace,
Muttering tunes with a smiling face.
"I'm slow but steady, watch me glide!"
Yet ended up in a mudslide.

With sparkly snacks tucked in their packs,
They held a feast by the train tracks.
Bananas flew, and giggles soared,
Under the moonlight, joy was stored.

As dawn approached, their pride did swell,
For laughter was magic; all could tell.
With newfound friends, they faced each day,
In every moment, the fun would play.

Radiant Reverie

In the land where socks lack pairs,
I found a treasure, a shoe full of flares.
With hats that dance and spoons that sing,
Life's silly moments are a wondrous thing.

A cat in a cape, with dreams so grand,
Rides on a bike, isn't that just grand?
With laughter as bright as a disco ball,
We chuckle and tumble, we won't let fall!

A whirl in the park with friends of glee,
Finding odd trinkets 'neath the old oak tree.
Puddles of giggles, splashes of cheer,
In a world filled with fun, we've nothing to fear!

With each silly twist and a playful glance,
Life sparkles more, gives absurdity a chance.
Every laugh a treasure, every jest a prize,
We'll dance through the days, with bright, eager eyes.

The Glistening Way

On paths of glitter, we wander around,
Stumbling on jellybeans strewn on the ground.
With shoes made of foam and shirts full of snacks,
We skip over sidewalk cracks, giggling acts.

A llama in sunglasses struts down the street,
With dance moves so silly, it's hard not to tweet.
As bubbles float by, we chase with delight,
Our laughter like fireworks, soaring in flight.

Pineapples wearing bow ties wave at the sun,
Claiming we're late, but we're already having fun.
With every odd sight, we treasure our quest,
In a world of absurd, we simply invest!

So let's grab a spoon and don our best hats,
Join in on the fun with our merry chitchats.
Each giggle a journey, through humor we sway,
Life's a bright carnival, come dance in the fray.

Journey Through Color

Roaming through rainbows on unicycle rides,
With jellyfish hats, and polka dot slides.
A squirrel in a tutu, a fox with a grin,
Every hue of laughter makes us feel like kin.

Grapes in sunglasses roll down the lane,
Chasing their dreams and dancing in the rain.
With cotton candy clouds and a pie in the sky,
We'll leap through the puddles where marshmallows lie.

Each color distinct, a palette of cheer,
Even broccoli sings when the party is near.
With laughter like paint, we splash all around,
In a world of the wacky, pure joy can be found.

So grab your bright crayons, let's doodle away,
In this world of whimsy, we'll laugh and we'll play.
Every giggle a brushstroke, bold and so true,
Creating a canvas of hues just for you.

The Amber Ascent

Climbing uphill with a bouncy ball,
Wearing mismatched socks, we're having a ball.
With each little stumble and slide on the rocks,
We giggle through life like a box full of clocks.

A dragon on roller skates skims by on the path,
Making the sun smile, oh do the math!
With donuts as wheels and giggles as fuel,
Life's silly adventures are our golden rule.

The breeze whispers secrets in ear of delight,
As we dance our way up, from morning to night.
Every step a wonder, each turn a surprise,
We chuckle and tumble, with shimmies and sighs.

And when we reach high with a cheer and a grin,
We'll toast to the silly and let the fun begin!
For life's a grand voyage, a whimsical play,
Where laughter and joy light our glittering way.

Luminescence and Lore

In a land where sparkles roam,
A chicken wore a diamond comb.
With every step, it clucked with glee,
Chasing light like a bumblebee.

A cat in pearls danced on the street,
Stumbling over its fancy feet.
Laughter echoed from trees so grand,
As squirrels held a treasure stand.

Far away in a town of glee,
A pirate searched for his lost key.
But it turned out to be a snack,
A gold-wrapped chocolate treasure pack!

With each new bite, a tale was spun,
Of silly ships and a sneaky bun.
The key was chocolate, who'd have thought?
Now that's the treasure that he sought!

Tides of Radiance

A crab in shades, quite the delight,
Danced on the shore, oh what a sight!
With sequined claws, it stole the scene,
Waving to fish like a festive queen.

The waves laughed hard, splashing around,
As seaweed sang with a bubbly sound.
A clam whispered jokes to the tide,
While sea stars twinkled, filled with pride.

Among the splashes, a dolphin spry,
Wore a necklace made of pie in the sky.
It twirled and flipped, oh what a show,
With tasty moonbeams in glorious flow!

But as night fell, the tide grew shy,
The dolphin's pie began to dry.
Yet laughter echoed through the bay,
As waves shared secrets of the day!

Secrets of the Shimmering Trail

A llama draped in silver bling,
Trotted along, ready to sing.
With every step, it dropped a charm,
Making all the critters swarm!

A hedgehog wore a ruby hat,
Said, "Now watch me roll like that!"
But it rolled too far, away it sped,
Tangled in a twinkly thread.

A parrot perched atop a stone,
Flapped its wings and squeaked, "You'll never be alone!"

At every loop, it cracked a joke,
Sending giggles through the oak.

As night approached, they gathered 'round,
The llama shared tales of what they found.
With laughter bubbling like a brook,
Their shining secrets read like a book!

Whispers of Hidden Wonders

Beneath a mushroom, secrets lie,
A snail in jewels waved goodbye.
It crept away with a flashy trail,
Leaving behind a sparkly veil.

A frog with feathers croaked a tune,
Dressed for a party under the moon.
His disco moves made flowers sway,
As insects joined in the lively fray.

A beetle wearing shades so bright,
Said, "I'm the DJ, let's dance tonight!"
With every beat, the night took flight,
Creating wonders, pure delight!

With laughter rising like morning dew,
They shared their dreams, both old and new.
In that hidden world, so full of cheer,
The whispers tangled like ribbons near!

Unveiling Hidden Splendors

In a garden where daisies wore crowns,
Laughter danced with each silly sound.
The sun blushed at flowers so grand,
As bees did the cha-cha, a hilarious band.

A squirrel stole acorns, thought they were gold,
He juggled them proudly, quite bold.
A clip on his tail, the audience roared,
He tripped and rolled—his act, adored!

The clouds dressed in cotton candy shawls,
Dropping candy instead of raindrops and squalls.
Giggling winds played tag with the grass,
Nature's circus, a splendid farce!

So much fun in this hidden scene,
Where laughter reigns, and all is serene.
Under trees, in this playful spree,
Life twinkles like gems, joyous and free.

A Tapestry of Colors and Roads

A rainbow once tried to find its hue,
It ended up tangled in an old shoe.
Worms threw a party, all wild and bright,
Dancing in mud, oh what a sight!

The sun wore sunglasses, thinking it cool,
While clouds wrote checks for puddles at school.
Raindrops laughed as they slid down the lane,
Squeaking in joy—life's silly refrain!

We traveled in socks, with mismatched shoes,
Cracked a few jokes, laughed at the blues.
All the paths turned to laughter and fun,
As we raced with the wind, hearts all as one.

So here's to the colors we stumbled upon,
Each road a punchline, from dusk until dawn.
With giggles and smiles on this winding track,
We treasure the moments, there's no looking back.

The Radiance of Untold Stories

A cat once wore a feathered hat,
Claiming it gave him a wise spat.
He purred loud tales of mice and cheese,
While squirrels nearby laughed with such ease.

At twilight, a frog recited his rhymes,
As fireflies blinked in sync to the chimes.
Adventures unfolded on lily pad stages,
With applause from the crowd, spanning all ages.

The trees whispered secrets of days ever bright,
While gnomes traded tales, laughing all night.
A dragon in pajamas shared stories of loot,
His treasure? A cupcake, quite a silly pursuit!

So let's spin a yarn in this whimsical glow,
Where laughter and tales forever flow.
Each moment a gem, sparkling anew,
In our hearts, those stories forever imbue.

Echoes of Gilded Footprints

With footprints in glitter, we danced on the sand,
Chasing the sunlight, hand in hand.
A crab in a top hat joined in the fun,
Declaring the beach a grand place to run!

We found seashells that whispered big dreams,
While jellyfish wiggled, bursting with beams.
The waves took selfies, splashing with cheer,
Creating a splash zone that everyone feared!

With buckets of laughter and shovels of smiles,
We built castles that reached heavenly miles.
Each turret adorned with a wild overstate,
As we laughed and danced—oh, what a fate!

So here's to the footsteps on sandy bright shores,
Where echoes of joy keep opening doors.
In the lightness we find, like grains in the breeze,
We treasure the moments, oh yes, with great ease!

A Journey through Light

I packed my bags with socks and pies,
Hoping to chase a golden surprise.
But tripped on a stone and fell in a stream,
Now I sparkle, or so it would seem.

I met a frog who wore a crown,
He claimed he was the best in town.
We danced a jig under a tree,
He said, "Join me, it's fun and carefree!"

The sun shone bright, my hat flew away,
Caught in the wind, it chose to play.
A squirrel snatched it with a laugh,
Now it's in style, my hapless gaffe.

So here's to travels, both wild and absurd,
Finding treasure in each silly word.
With every stumble, I learn and grow,
My radiant journey, a well-lit show!

The Luminous Pathway

On a bright path lined with bright-eyed ants,
I wore my shoes, not knowing my dance.
I slipped on a banana, did a spin,
The world started laughing, how could I win?

A talking cactus offered advice,
He said, "Travel light, pack only some spice.
Forget the maps, just follow your nose,
To places where the silly wind blows!"

I met a bird with a glittery tail,
He sang me a song of an odd, wacky whale.
We twirled and we laughed till the sun set low,
In the glow of colors, we started to glow.

So here's to pathways filled with mirth,
Chasing laughter, the best kind of worth.
With each silly step, I find my delight,
In this quirky adventure, everything's bright!

Reflections on the Road

I looked in a puddle, saw a goat with a tie,
He winked and said, 'I can leap, oh my!'
But when I tried, I just fell flat,
Now I'm known as the queen of splat!

I wandered down paths with marshmallow trees,
Where candy confetti floated in the breeze.
A worm shouted, 'Hey, look at me shine!'
I thought, 'That's odd, but it's all fine!'

A chipmunk in shades said, 'Join my parade!'
I danced with my shadow, a weird charade.
The pie I ate, it seemed to dance,
Became my partner in this silly prance.

So cheers to the moments, unexpected, absurd,
Where every misstep creates a new word.
In this laughter-filled adventure, I surely reside,
With all my friends, what a wild ride!

Fantasia of Facets

In a carnival bright, with colors ablaze,
I tried to juggle with one hand in a daze.
A pompous parrot squawked, 'What a sight!
You may just win the clown's delight!'

I pirouetted past a horse on a bike,
"Is this even real?" I wondered, "What's the hype?"
But he chuckled and said, "Join in the fun,
Together we shine, we've only begun!"

We whirled through the stalls, full of whimsy and cheer,
Each facet of laughter, I held so dear.
A badge of silliness pinned to my chest,
In this fantasy world, I felt truly blessed.

So here's to the moments that sparkle and gleam,
With laughter and friendship, a whimsical dream.
In this dazzle of facets, I dance through life's show,
With every giggle, my joy starts to grow!

Hearts of Glass and Gold

In a market bright, a sparkly haul,
A lady slipped, dropped her crystal ball.
"Ouch!" she exclaimed, the crowd in a hush,
As beads rolled away in a wild little rush.

Her treasures gleamed, a wild little spree,
But one cheeky gem danced off with glee.
A seagull swooped down, fancy on a quest,
To steal the glittery prize from the rest!

With everyone gasping, she shouted, "Just wait!"
As gems flew like birds, oh, wasn't that great?
A shop full of sparkles, and laughter galore,
Who knew a market could lead to such roar?

Heart of glass or a heart full of cheer,
Either way, the fun draws us near.
With laughter and gems, let both worlds collide,
In a shimmering crowd where no one can hide.

The Mysterious Radiance

A bright little rock sat on a tall shelf,
It winked at a boy who couldn't help himself.
He thought, "What a find! A treasure so rare!"
Yet it was just an old marble, strung with despair.

With a twist and a turn, he gave it a toss,
A whirlwind of sparkles, and then chaos!
The dogs all barked, the cat stole the flare,
While the boy chased sunbeams, without a care.

In the jumble and tumble, the marble did gleam,
As shadows swooped in like a mischievous dream.
"Watch out!" yelled a girl, with a playful grin,
As the gang of bright stones began to spin!

Together they danced, a raucous affair,
Creating new stories, spinning out their flair.
In the end, the old marble just smiled with pride,
For even old trinkets can glow from inside.

The Glimmering Quest

A thief with a cap, his pockets quite deep,
Set off on a quest, no time for sleep.
He sought shiny trinkets atop every hill,
Yet tripped on a rock, oh what a thrill!

As he rolled down, collecting all loot,
He found a bright button that looked like a fruit.
"Not gold, but it shines like a beacon of fun!"
He laughed to himself, a true shining one.

With squirrels as his crew and birds in a line,
He crafted a crown—what a glorious sign!
In the end, the treasures were sillier still,
As they bantered and bragged on a powdery hill.

So this quest, quite absurd, for treasure or glee,
Led to laughter and songs, as wild as can be.
For in the great search, what really does gleam,
Are the bonds that we build, more than gold or a dream.

Wanderlust's Lattice

In a glitzy bazaar where colors would clash,
A girl laced her hat with a rainbow splash.
With trinkets and baubles, her style so insane,
She twirled like a peacock, oh, what a gain!

Through alleyways bright, with laughter and cheer,
She juggled her finds, spreading good vibes here.
An errant banana peel led to a slip,
But her treasures flew high on the twirl of a trip.

With each wobbly step, she gathered a crew,
All clutching their hats, their sparkle anew.
With every mishap, they'd laugh with delight,
In the weave of the day, everything felt right.

At dusk they would dance under starry confetti,
Where wandering hearts felt wild and ready.
So remember, dear friend, in your search for a gain,
The best of the finds are the times that remain.

Prism of the Traveler's Soul

In a suitcase, socks collide,
A map of chaos, wild and wide,
Lost my way but not my smile,
Each detour brings a brand new style.

With mismatched shoes, I roam so free,
Sipping tea with a bumblebee,
A sightseer with pancakes stacked,
On this road, I'm fully packed.

The compass laughs, points to a tree,
'Go that way,' it giggles with glee,
I trip on roots and tumble down,
Found a treasure, a jester's crown!

In laughter, I find my way back,
Life's a circus, I'm on the track,
With glittering dreams to light the night,
Adventure's the gem that feels just right.

The Allure of Untamed Paths

I wander where the wild things roam,
Grass stains make my heart feel home,
Chasing squirrels in my raincoat bright,
Each splatter of mud, pure delight.

In tangled vines and buzzing bees,
I barter jokes, I trade with ease,
An old shoe here, a sock over there,
Fashion's lost but who will care?

A hiccup from the ginger ale,
Onward I go, with my grand tale,
Lollipop sticks, my hiking poles,
A tapestry stitched with silly rolls.

The horizon winks, 'Come take a look,'
Each turn I take, a brand new book,
Forever searching for chuckles and cheer,
In nature's laughter, I feel no fear.

Luminous Threads of Memory

Knitting tales in the summer sun,
Each yarn a laugh, each stitch pure fun,
Purls of joy, a spooling thread,
In my hat, a small bird's wed.

She says, "Oh look, it's mismatched flair!"
I nod and twirl with flowy hair,
Through tangled fibers, we dance and spin,
With every snicker, we weave joy in.

Remember that time we brewed some tea?
We spilled on the cat, oh, what a spree!
A golden mishap, a glorious gift,
In clumsy moments, our spirits lift.

These threads hold giggles, tears, and smiles,
A fabric of friendship that stretches miles,
Wrapped in memory, warm and bright,
Every stitch sings, 'What a delight!'

Secrets Buried in the Soil

Digging deep where secrets lie,
With a trowel and a curious eye,
Found a sandwich, half-eaten bliss,
A relic of a picnic I wouldn't miss.

In garden beds where weeds take flight,
I dance with worms into the night,
Each root I pull, a tale to share,
"Why did the carrot cross? To get somewhere!"

I unearthed a gnome, quite a sight,
With a wobbly grin, he joins the flight,
Together we plot, oh what a scheme,
To plant more giggles in the stream.

Between the pebbles, I laugh and play,
With muddy hands, I greet the day,
In every scoop, a chuckle's spun,
In this earthy treasure, we're forever one.

The Opal Odyssey

In a land where colors sing,
A purple pig took to the wing,
He stumbled on a shiny rock,
And danced around the ticking clock.

A cat in glasses joined the chase,
Declared that gems had lost their grace,
With every leap, he lost his hat,
And laughed aloud, 'How about that!'

A giant frog in sequined shoes,
Held court to all his wobbly crews,
They juggled sticks and made a mess,
In this wild world, they found success.

At last they stopped to take a break,
While reindeer baked a ginger cake,
With icing gems that sparkled bright,
They feasted under the moonlight.

Glittering Routes

On a path where shadows play,
A rabbit baked his dreams all day,
With icing made from kale and thyme,
He thought he'd changed his life with rhyme.

A turtle raced at lightning speed,
While bouncing on a pogo reed,
They found a treasure chest with snacks,
And danced around like silver backs.

A lion wore a paper crown,
While wearing socks of purple brown,
His majesty beside the cheese,
Made all the critters giggle with ease.

The journey led to party tunes,
With singing frogs and clumsy loons,
They hopped and popped beneath the sun,
And called it fun, 'We've surely won!'

Each glittered stone, a memory made,
In goofy hats, they danced and played,
With smiles as bright as every shade,
In this wild world, all worries fade.

Stones beneath the Stars

A raccoon believed in cosmic fate,
He skated on a figure-eight,
With rocks that sparkled in the night,
He leaped and twirled with pure delight.

A squirrel wore a tiny cape,
He thought he'd found the perfect shape,
With every flip, he'd drop a nut,
And giggle loud when things would cut.

A wise old owl haphazardly flew,
In search of gems that he once knew,
He stumbled on some glittering dust,
And lost his way, but laughed, 'In rust we trust!'

They gathered 'neath the moonlit glow,
With stories of adventures slow,
Each stone a fragment of their laughs,
Creating maps of silly crafts.

In this vast universe of play,
Where brilliance sparkles every day,
They turned their dreams into a show,
And made a wish on stars that glow.

The Sapphire Sojourn

A gnome with shoes of polka dots,
Set off to find what tied the knots,
With laughter bursting from his chest,
He skipped along, never at rest.

A chubby bear in stripes of blue,
Sang silly songs to all the crew,
They wobbled down a winding trail,
Trading stories that would never fail.

A dragon danced to quirky beats,
While rolling on two tiny feet,
His sparkling scales drew quite the crowd,
They cheered him on, so bold and loud.

They reached a grove with trees of gold,
Exchanging tales of riches bold,
With every joke and playful tease,
They celebrated with great ease.

In this wild spree of carefree fun,
Under a warm and friendly sun,
A journey shared with silly hearts,
Turned every gem into fine arts.

The Celestial Memento

There once was a star, it was quite a sight,
It danced in the sky, brightening the night.
But trip over a comet, oh what a blunder,
Chasing it down, with a laugh and a thunder.

With a wink and a twirl, it spun out of reach,
The cosmic jester, it taught me to teach.
Forget all the worries, just follow the spark,
Life's just a show, and you're part of the lark.

In a pocket of air, I found quite a thing,
A wish-granting pebble, or so they did sing.
I tossed it in skits, and pretended it worked,
But all it did do was make me a nerd!

So here's to the stars, and their silly old dance,
They twirl and they prance, do give them a chance.
For laughter, it sparkles, and shines oh-so bright,
In the grand cosmic theater, it's pure delight.

A Treetop of Baubles

Up high in a tree, where the sunlight does gleam,
A squirrel found treasures, or so it would seem.
With acorns and marbles, he thought he was rich,
But his stash turned to chaos, oh, what a hitch!

He gathered the trinkets and made quite a scene,
His treasure map led to a shimmering bean.
Thought of it as golden, a true pot of cheer,
But it fizzled and popped, gave him quite a fear!

In search for more sparkles, he climbed really high,
But slipped on a leaf, oh me, oh my!
He tumbled and rolled, with a squeak and a shout,
In a pile of bright pebbles, he chuckled about.

Now that little squirrel, in the tree above,
Holds concerts for critters, gotten rid of the glove.
For laughter's the prize, and living's the goal,
A pocketful of fun is the heart of the soul.

The Sun-Kissed Journey

With sandals untied, I set off to roam,
The sun kissed my brow, I felt right at home.
Through puddles I splashed, oh, watch out for that,
A frog on a lily, or was it a cat?

I tripped on a skateboard, it rolled with a grin,
A parade of wild flavors began to spin.
With ice cream that juggled and pop corn that danced,
Every step was a giggle, I pranced and pranced.

In the land of bright bubbles, I lost all my grace,
A tumble and wiggle, oh look at this place!
With confetti in pockets and laughter in air,
I forgot where I started, just floated without care.

Now I carry that sunshine, wherever I tread,
With giggles like sunshine, I'm never misled.
For life's just a journey, wearing such glee,
As we paint the world bright, just you and me!

A Collection of Reflections

I peeked in a puddle, oh what did I see?
A squirrel in a hat, laughing back up at me!
With a wink and a nod, it danced like a pro,
And I joined in some jig, what a marvelous show!

A mirror of mischief, it caught all my tricks,
A walrus named Winston offered snacks on some sticks.
We chewed through the laughter, with crumbs on our beards,
Swapping our stories, just sharing our weirds.

Then I asked old Winston, "What's the secret to fun?"
He chuckled so deeply, "Just be on the run!
Collect all the giggles, and the happy mistakes,
For joy's in the journey, it's the path that it takes!"

So I'll chase down the ripples, and dance with great flair,
In a world full of wonders, I'll leap without care.
For life's just a mirror, reflecting a dream,
With laughter's sweet echo, together we beam.

Gems Beyond the Horizon

In a land where socks go to hide,
A glittering rock joined the ride.
It danced on the screen, oh such a delight,
But rolled off the table, out of sight.

The cat thought it looked like a treat,
Pawed it around with quick little feet.
As I chased it down with a jump and a slide,
We both ended up in a tumble, what a ride!

Under the couch, it sparkled and shone,
While I grumbled and searched for my phone.
A treasure, I thought, from a jokingly deep sack,
Turns out it's just my old dog's snack!

With laughter we both connected the dots,
Trading our finds, my new gem for her socks.
In the end, it's the moments we gain,
That make every silly chase feel sane.

The Luster of Lost Trails

At dawn, I set out with pockets so wide,
For a shiny trinket and a fun-filled ride.
But I tripped on a root, fell flat on my rear,
A squirrel just snickered, 'Your trinket's not here!'

With a map that was drawn by a toddler in haste,
I stumbled through woods with zero good taste.
Every turn that I took led me straight to a pond,
Where fish wore tiny hats, oh my, how they dawned!

I met a wise turtle who claimed to know all,
He said, 'It's your humor that makes you stand tall.'
So I laughed with the frogs and the bumblebees too,
And forgot all about that shiny thing, boo-hoo!

With sparkles in laughter and giggles in the air,
I found the real treasure—in joy and in care.
Not a gem but a grin, shining all through the day,
As I waddled back home, all muddy and gay.

Radiant Paths of Discovery

In search of a treasure, I donned my best gear,
With a compass that spun, I held it so near.
But the map was upside-down; what a comical scene,
Was I headed for the mountains or the land of cuisine?

I followed a rabbit who danced with delight,
Leading me straight to a pizza take flight.
With toppings like diamonds, tomatoes gone wild,
I pondered if flavor is really that styled?

A journey it seemed, like a pie in the sky,
With laughter and cheese that made my heart fly.
In the end, I discovered that real is the fun,
Not just the prize, but a feast for everyone!

So here's to the path that makes us all giggle,
With each silly step, our joy will all wiggle.
The laughter and moments, they truly impart,
A treasure so deep, in the depths of the heart.

Shimmering Echoes in the Mist

On a foggy day with my friend by my side,
We searched for glimmers, oh what a wild ride!
Through bramble and thicket we stumbled, confused,
Found a shiny old shoe that was surely abused!

It sparkled with promise and stories untold,
Of adventures past, and the bravery bold.
A king might have tripped, or a prince lost his luck,
All we could do was giggle and cluck!

We forged on ahead with our newfound 'treasure',
With each silly thought measuring laughter's pure pleasure.
A voice in the breeze said, 'How funny indeed,
That the wildest journeys are where fun takes the lead!'

The mist wrapped around us, soft as a hug,
As we filled our hearts with this whimsical drug.
With shimmering memories, we danced through the lore,
Finding joy in the searching, who could ask for more?

The Golden Horizon

A treasure map marked with crumbs,
X never leads where the gold hums.
Sailing on teacups, what a sight,
Who knew the ocean held so much light?

Dancing with seagulls, they steal my fries,
Plot twist, they're experts in disguise.
Capsize the boat? Oh please, not today,
I've got a fish to catch, come what may!

The sun's a coin that's flipped in the sky,
I'm just a pirate with a pie and a sigh.
Buried rum under a palm so neat,
History's wild; look out for the heat!

A seagull squawks, "Where's my bling?"
I toss him a shell, it's not quite the thing.
Adventure awaits with a wink and a grin,
But watch out for waves—now let's begin!

A Starlit Voyage

Sailing past puns in a cosmic sea,
Martian fish wink, saying, "Join me, please!"
Wept for the moon, it's a lopsided sight,
Chasing starfish that dance in the night.

Floating on laughter, no compass in hand,
I barter with aliens for pizza and sand.
Shooting stars leave trails of whipped cream,
Who knew the sky was a giant dream?

Glimmers of giggles bounce off the waves,
Octopus jesters in glittery caves.
Their jokes are quite fishy, but I laugh aloud,
Riding the tides with a slapstick crowd.

Then a comet whizzes, with a wink and a cheer,
"Buy one, get one on space travel here!"
Buckle up, folks, it's a riotous ride,
In the universe's antics, I take great pride!

The Velvet Voyage

A carpet so plush, we float above ground,
Horses made of marshmallows trot all around.
Jellybean rivers, oh what a treat,
Look out for the gumdrops, they'll sweep you off your feet!

Riding on giggles through clouds made of fluff,
"More marshmallows!" I shout; this ride's never tough.
Rainbows pour sprinkles, a colorful flare,
Unicorns prance while I'm combing my hair.

Beware of the trolls with their silly old songs,
They'll challenge your dance moves, or play tricks that are wrong.
With every misstep, we tumble and roll,
But that's just the magic of this velvet stroll!

We eventually land, but not quite on grass,
In a field of cupcakes, oh what a class!
So here we munch, giggling through the day,
A velvet ride finished with icing and play!

Into the Heart of Opulence

Glittery roads paved with candy canes,
Dodging the hiccups of sugar-sweet trains.
At tea with the queen, we sip from dolls' cups,
Her corgis wear crowns; what an odd bunch!

A diamond from donuts rolls past my feet,
Cakes of a castle, merriment's treat.
What's next on the menu? A snack from the throne,
Waffles with syrup that sparkles and moans.

The jesters juggle with gummy bears bright,
Chortling and chuckling, it's pure delight.
In this lavish life where the silly is grand,
We laugh and we twirl, no need for a plan.

Bonkers adventures await every day,
In this heart of fancy, we frolic and sway.
So take off your shoes, let your worries all cease,
For in this absurdity, we find our peace!

Along the Bejeweled Way

I tripped on a diamond, oh what a sight,
A sparkle that flashed in the midday light.
My friend laughed so hard, almost fell on the ground,
He picked up the gem, then spun it around.

A ruby rolled past like a runaway car,
We chased it for blocks, what a bizarre bazaar.
It led us to laughter, we named it Bertie,
And took it to dinner, oh wasn't that dirty!

We found a lost emerald, deep in a tree,
A squirrel claimed it first, said, "This is for me!"
We bartered with nuts, and a piece of pie,
That squirrel, oh so wise, gave us a goodbye.

And so we have tales from our wild, funny hunt,
With treasures and giggles, like jokes that aren't blunt.
So if you should wander on this silly run,
Pack snacks for the critters; just go have some fun!

The Chromatic Trek

Through valleys of color, we pranced with delight,
A parade of odd trinkets that shone oh so bright.
A calico cat wore a necklace of pearls,
With hip, jivey moves, it danced and it twirls.

Our hats were adorned with lost bits of flair,
We giggled at treasures that floated in air.
A toucan squawked, sporting a bright azure gem,
Said, "Keep it, my friends, you have plenty of them!"

We stumbled on gold, a fine tasty treat,
Beneath all the glitz, was a banquet to eat.
Each bite was a joy, with a twist and a crunch,
Who knew a donut could give such a punch?

We laughed till we cried at the strange things we found,
With colors so vivid, our hearts knew no bound.
This journey of hues, oh, we'd do it again,
With flavors and wisecracks, through sun and through rain!

Echoes of Elegance

In a ballroom of giggles, we danced in a haze,
With twinkling attire that dazzled for days.
A monocle fell from a posh little chap,
As he tripped on his coat; oh, what a mishap!

A crown made of gummy bears sparkled with glee,
While confetti rained down, like it was a spree.
The butler spilled punch, in a comical mess,
As we dove for the snacks, you couldn't care less.

Amidst all the humor, an old clock chimed loud,
We laughed at its style, oh, what a proud crowd!
They swayed and they slipped in the most lovely way,
Stilettos and giggles made for a grand play.

So here's to the echoes of laughter and cheer,
In elegance twisted, with no space for fear.
We wore not just jewels, oh not even a trace,
Just humor and fun, in this shimmering place!

Treasures Untold

A map made of chocolate led us to loot,
With sprinkles and fudge, the best treasure to boot.
But a marshmallow monster guarded it tight,
We offered him gum, and he giggled in spite.

A pearl-clad penguin showed us the way,
He waddled and pranced, brightening the day.
We asked him for wisdom, he shrugged with delight,
"Just enjoy every nibble, it's all about the bite!"

We stumbled on tokens, from fairs way back when,
A rubber duck army, yelling, "Join us, my friend!"
We leaped and we laughed, as they bounced on the ground,
Finding fun in the smallest, the joy that we found.

So here's to the wonders, the giggles bought gold,
With stories a-plenty and friendships to fold.
In treasure so silly; what's better to hold,
Than moments of laughter, priceless and bold?

Treasures Found in Wandering

In a pocket, I found old snacks,
A map led me to some sweet waxed backs.
Laughed at the shiny, my fortune's in crumbs,
Chasing down laughter, oh, how it hums!

With every misstep, a smile on my face,
Tripping on treasures, this silly old race.
My GPS misled, took me straight to a clown,
Where laughter's the gold; no need for a crown!

Sticky notes left by the roadside appear,
Reminders of fun, oh, the joy's always near.
In the wildest of hunts, I hear giggles unfold,
What's better than gold? A tale to be told!

So join me, dear friends, for a stroll or a dance,
The weirdest adventures await in a glance.
With pockets full of smiles, and hearts light as air,
We'll chase after chuckles, with nothing to spare!

The Map of Hidden Glories

Oh, a parchment I found with scribbles galore,
Promising treasures behind every door.
But directions led me to socks without mates,
And a garden of gnomes who love to debate!

With a compass that spins like a top on its head,
I wandered in circles, ate jelly instead.
Searching for fortunes marked 'X' on a hill,
I discovered a dog who just wanted to chill!

A treasure of cookies from strangers I met,
Each smile was a gem, like a lifetime's vignette.
With giggles and hugs, we shared tea made of grass,
Who knew such riches could come from the sass?

So join this grand quest for the laughter to glean,
For the path lined with fun is the best there's been seen.
This treasure map's best with good pals by your side,
In the land of the silly, let's take a wild ride!

Glimmering Trails of the Heart

Bouncing along, my heart's in a spin,
Finding lost things where laughter begins.
A pebble that sparkles, it rolled with a grin,
It whispered sweet tales of where it had been!

Underneath benches, I spotted a shoe,
A mystery paired with a wild kangaroo!
Stumbling through bumbles, I found a lost friend,
Together we giggled, the fun had no end!

Golden moments pop up like stars in the night,
In the laughter of children, I find pure delight.
With every quirky step, my joy's on the rise,
In this treasure hunt, laughter is the prize!

So pack up your heart and let's dance down the lane,
With winding paths leading to joy without pain.
A journey of giggles, let's travel afar,
Chasing our dreams like the sun and a star!

Stones of Wisdom on the Way

Tripping over pebbles, my wisdom grows strange,
Each bumpy little rock has a giggle to exchange.
Wandered through puddles made by cats in the rain,
Where every splash echoes and joy's not in vain!

A wise old turtle offered me sage,
"Life's about laughs!" wrote on a cool page.
With each ponderous step, he led me to wonder,
"To seek the goofy, and skip all the blunders!"

Loads of odd socks piled high like a hill,
Remind me of fun, oh, what a thrill!
I gather the quirks like stones in a sack,
With laughter as currency, there's no looking back!

So come, my dear friends, let's wander this path,
Where giggles and grins are the aftermath.
For in silly moments and joy as we roam,
We build our own treasure, our hearts, our real home!

Treasures of the Heart

In a pocket of laughter, I keep my charms,
Curious knick-knacks, no need for alarms.
A toothpick from lunch, a button so bright,
My treasures of giggles, a pure delight.

From lost socks to baubles, my stash has no end,
Each tells a story, each has a friend.
A rubber band ball, an old fuzzy cat,
Who knew such odd wonders would make me so fat?

A mismatched sock dance, I prance in delight,
With treasures that sparkle, all fluffy and light.
In the jumbles of thumbtacks and old paper clips,
I find my delight in these comical flips.

So gather your trinkets, your bits and your bobs,
Embrace all the chaos, with laughter, no sobs.
Your heart can be full of the weird and the wacky,
In the treasure chest of life, it's all super tacky.

Shimmering Destinations

Off to a place where my snacks shine bright,
With chips on my shoulder, I'll take a big bite.
A flight made of cookies, my stomach's the guide,
Who knew that dessert could fit in a ride?

I dream of a world made of candy and cream,
Where gumdrops grow tall, and rivers just stream.
With lollipops rising like mountains of cheer,
Every step a giggle, with nothing to fear.

A castle of waffles, its towers so sweet,
With syrupy lakes where the marshmallows greet.
In a land of pure fun, I happily roam,
With jellybean friends, I'll never feel alone.

So paint your adventures with colors so bold,
In this funny realm, just let the day unfold.
With laughter as riches, and joy as my quest,
I'll treasure each moment, it's truly the best.

The Amethyst Adventure

In a world made of purple, I trek with a grin,
With grapes on my head, where do I begin?
I skipped past some rabbits in top hats so tall,
Who pointed at puddles made out of sprawl.

The rocks all were laughing, they tumbled and rolled,
As I danced with a wizard, or so I was told.
He offered me potions that glittered like suns,
But all that I wanted were soft cinnamon buns.

I tripped on a diamond, slipped into a joke,
Bounced back like a spring, "I'm no ordinary bloke!"
With each step I cackled, the gems shouted back,
"Join our sparkling party, we'll keep on the track!"

So if you should stumble on amethyst streams,
Remember to laugh, live life in your dreams.
For in every adventure where giggles are chime,
There's joy in the purple, oh, what a good time!

Voyage of Vibrance

Set sail on a ship made of bright maraschino,
With colors ablaze, like a funky casino.
We'll trade jokes with dolphins and giggles with clowns,
As we skip over waves in our bright polka-dots gowns.

The captain's a fruitcake, a real crazy chap,
With a pirate's eye patch and a permanent nap.
He laughs at the seagulls who squawk with delight,
And plays peek-a-boo with the sun through the night.

We'll dive for some treasures, oh what could they be?
A hat made of pizza? A sponge in a tree?
With each funny moment, we gather new smiles,
In this vibrant escape, we'll sail for a while.

So grab all your rainbows, your giggles, your glee,
Our voyage of color is wild, wait and see!
With laughter as currency, let's sail through the fun,
In the world of vibrance, we'll shine like the sun.

www.ingramcontent.com/pod-product-compliance
Lightning Source LLC
Chambersburg PA
CBHW062111280426
43661CB00086B/450